The Biggest Snowball of All

by Jane Belk Moncure
illustrated by Joy Friedman

Published by

THE CHILD'S WORLD®

Mankato, Minnesota

GROLIER BOOKS

Grolier Books is a division of
Grolier Enterprises, Inc.,
Danbury, CT.

The Library —
A Magic Castle

Come to the magic castle
When you are growing tall.
Rows upon rows of Word Windows
Line every single wall.
They reach up high,
As high as the sky,
And you want to open them all.
For every time you open one,
A new adventure has begun.

Emily opened a Word
Window. Here is what
she read.

One day Little Bear made a tiny snowball.

"This snowball is so small, it will fit on the end of my nose," she said.

She put the snowball on her nose and

down

the snowy hill she went. But . . .

the snowball did not stay on her nose
for long. It fell off . . .

and rolled down the hill.

As it rolled, it grew bigger . . .

and bigger . . .

and bigger.

"Stop," cried Little Bear.

But the snowball rolled on down the
hill until . . .

it bumped into Raccoon.

"What a big snowball," Raccoon said.
"It will make a fine head for a snowbear."

"Good idea," said Little Bear.

The two friends went right to work.
They made a bigger snowball for the
middle of the snowbear . . .

and another snowball for the bottom
of the snowbear. It was the biggest
snowball of the three.

Then they put all three snowballs together.

"What a fine snowbear," they said.

Just then Rabbit came down the hill on her sled.

"Watch out!" she cried.

Little Bear and Raccoon jumped away.
But Rabbit bumped into the snowbear.

Bump! Bump!

Off rolled the snowbear's head and . . .

down

the hill it went.

"Jump on my sled," said Rabbit. "We will catch it."

The three friends hopped on . . .

the smallest in front, and the biggest
in back. Away they went.

When they came to the bottom of
the hill, guess what they saw?

The
biggest
snowball
of all.

It was so big that Little Bear said,
"Let's build a snowball house."

They went right to work. Little Bear made
a wide door so they could get inside.

Raccoon and Rabbit made two narrow
windows so they could peek outside.

Then the three friends went inside
to play. They played for a long time.

While they were playing,
the sun came out.

The sun was hot. Guess what?

The biggest snowball
of all began to melt.

It grew smaller . . .

and smaller . . .

and even
smaller.

Soon the biggest snowball
of all . . .

was very, very small. It was so tiny . . .

that Little Bear said, "It will fit on the end of my nose."

And it did.

You can read these size words with
Little Bear.

tiny

small

big

bigger

even bigger

biggest of all!